CHRISTIE'S
COLLECTIBLES

CHRISTIE'S
COLLECTIBLES

ART DECO
CERAMICS

Jane Hay

A BULFINCH PRESS BOOK
LITTLE, BROWN AND COMPANY
BOSTON • NEW YORK • TORONTO • LONDON

First North American Edition

ISBN 0-8212-2271-6

Library of Congress Catalog Card Number 95-80529

EDITORS HEATHER MAGRILL, ISABELLA RAEBURN
DESIGNERS FRANCES DE REES, HELEN SPENCER
PICTURE EDITOR ELIZABETH LOVING

Marshall Editions would like to thank
Edward Schneider of Christie's Images for his help
in the creation of this book.

Conceived, edited, and designed by
Marshall Editions
170 Piccadilly London W1V 9DD

Bulfinch Press is an imprint and trademark of
Little, Brown and Company (Inc.)

Published simultaneously in Canada by
Little, Brown & Company (Canada) Limited

PRINTED IN PORTUGAL

CHRISTIE'S
502 Park Avenue New York NY 10022

CHRISTIE'S EAST
219 East 67th Street New York NY 10021

CHRISTIE'S CANADA
170 Bloor Street West Suite 210 Toronto Ontario M5S IT9

CHRISTIE'S
8 King Street St. James's London SW1Y 6QT

CHRISTIE'S SOUTH KENSINGTON
85 Old Brompton Road London SW7 3LD

CHRISTIE'S AUSTRALIA
298 New South Head Road Double Bay Sydney NSW 2028

CHRISTIE'S SOUTH AFRICA
P.O. Box 72126 Parkview Johannesburg 2122

CHRISTIE'S JAPAN
Sankyo Ginza Building 6-5-13 Ginza Chuo-ku Tokyo 104

Contents

INTRODUCTION 6
ASHTEAD POTTERY 12
BOCH FRÈRES 14
BURLEIGH 16
RENÉ BUTHAUD 18
CARLTON 19
CLARICE CLIFF 22
SUSIE COOPER 26
CROWN DEVON 30
FRENCH PORCELAIN 32
GERMAN POTTERY 34
GERMAN STONEWARE 35
GINORI 36
GOLDSCHEIDER 37
CARRUTHERS GOULD 39
GENEVIÈVE GRANGER 40
GUSTAVSBERG 41
HARRODS EXHIBITION 42
KATZHÜTTE THURINGIA 48
ROBERT LALLEMENT 49
LENCI 50

LIMOGES 52
LONGWY 53
MOORCROFT 54
KEITH MURRAY 55
POOLE POTTERY 56
CHARLOTTE RHEAD 58
ROSENTHAL 60
ROYAL COPENHAGEN 61
ROYAL DOULTON 62
SÈVRES 64
SHELLEY 66
JOHN SKEAPING 69
VI.BI. 70
WADE 71
LOUIS WAIN 72
WEDGWOOD 74
WIENER WERKSTÄTTE 76
FRANK LLOYD WRIGHT 77
GLOSSARY 78
INDEX 79
ACKNOWLEDGMENTS 80

PRICE CODES

The following price codes are used in this book:
\$A Less than \$150 **\$B** \$151–\$525
\$C \$526–\$750 **\$D** \$751–\$1,500 **\$E** \$1,501–\$2,250
\$F \$2,251–\$3,000 **\$G** More than \$3,000

Valuation is an imprecise art and prices can vary for many
reasons, including the condition of a piece, fashion, and national and
regional interest. Prices given in this book are approximate
and based on likely *auction* values. *Insurance* values reflect the
retail replacement price and as such are liable to be higher.

Introduction

$\mathcal{A}$ LIVELY STYLE COMBINING RICH DECORATION WITH geometric outline, Art Deco is properly defined as the style prevalent between the Paris Exhibition of 1925, which introduced the world to "l'Art Décoratif," and the outbreak of World War II, although examples on either side of these limits exist.

$\mathcal{T}$he 1925 Paris Exhibition, officially the "Exposition des Arts Décoratifs et Industriels Modernes," was part of a long tradition of international trade fairs designed to show off the best of modern design to the public and had an enormous impact on contemporary taste. Although it was dominated by the French, it was clear that a new mood was in the air internationally, with the

The pavilion of the Galeries Lafayette at the 1925 Paris Exhibition was one of the most original there.

The interior of the French trans-Atlantic liner
S.S. Normandie *shows Art Deco style at its height.*

organic free-flowing lines of Art Nouveau being replaced by geometric forms and rectilinear designs combined with sumptuous decorative techniques. The style was to reach its apogee a decade later with the launching of the French trans-Atlantic luxury liner S.S. *Normandie* in 1935. Furnished by leading designers, again mostly from France, the ship embodied all that was best in the Art Deco style.

*B*ut the French did not have a monopoly on Art Deco. It was a new look that swept the world, taking many forms and subject to many influences. The development of the film industry did much to popularize the new style. Indeed, there is a whole subsection of Art Deco known as the Odeon style, after the great movie theaters of the day which incorporated Sunburst and Egyptianesque motifs with abandon. The advent of the industrial machine age made an impact, as did new

The ballroom of the Park Lane Hotel, London, shows typically Art Deco motifs in its decoration.

forms of travel such as the airplane, which gave rise to dynamic forms associated with speed, notably in Italy where Futurism took hold.

*O*ther developments that contributed to the style were the discovery of Tutankhamun's tomb in 1922 and the interest which Cubist and Fauvist artists such as Picasso took in African art and sculpture. The emancipation of women, with shorter hairstyles and dresses, as well as the upsurge of jazz music, can often be seen in figurative studies from this period. So, too, can the craze for health that swept Europe after World War I: what can be more 1920s in style than a model of a young woman in a swimsuit carrying a parasol? Various earlier artists and designers were also extremely influential, among them Charles Rennie Mackintosh, one of the first to take up the rectilinear style; Frank Lloyd Wright; the Bauhaus in Germany; and Austria's Wiener Werkstätte.

The period between the wars was one of immense change, but not all of the new developments were positive. The Wall Street Crash of 1929 heralded the Depression, when people had little money to spend and certainly none for expensive luxury items. This resulted in simple, hard-wearing styles which could be made cheaply using the techniques of mass production.

Since Art Deco ceramics are relatively inexpensive and reflect the tremendous variety of the age – ranging from

William Van Alen's Chrysler Building in New York exploited Art Deco, even in its superb elevators.

cheap and cheerful to the height of luxury – it is possible to build a varied collection, even on a limited budget, and to derive great enjoyment from doing so.

TIPS FOR COLLECTORS

• Buy what you like and do not allow yourself to be deflected by others. If you become bored with a piece later, you can always sell it again; but if you pass up the opportunity to buy something, you may find that you regret it in years to come.

• Always buy the best that you can afford, especially with regard to condition. Often a piece that seems costly will gain in value over time and can prove to be an investment. Badly damaged or restored examples,

The fascination with jazz, common in the Art Deco era, is reflected in Clarice Cliff's "Age of Jazz" duo, c.1935.

The carpet of Radio City Music Hall, in Rockefeller Center, New York, shows images typical of the Jazz Age.

however, will not usually increase in value unless they are exceptionally rare to begin with.

• Take care when cleaning pieces: some decoration is oil based and will come off in detergent; scrubbing can lift off fragile on-glaze enamels; and a rapid change from hot to cold water can result in a nasty crack.

• Keep a record of your purchases. This is useful both for insurance purposes and if you decide to sell in the future. Check with your insurer the value above which pieces should be photographed and separately listed on your insurance.

• Stick to reputable auction houses and dealers. If you can build up a rapport with dealers and auction specialists and they get a feel for your taste, they can look out for pieces which may appeal to you. Only when you have gotten your feet wet in your particular field is it time to match your wits against the car trunk sale trader!

Ashtead Pottery I

BASED IN EPSOM,
England, Ashtead
Pottery was
established in 1923
by the philanthropists
Sir Lawrence and
Kathleen, Lady Weaver,
to provide employment
for disabled veterans
and their families after
World War I. At its height,
the pottery persuaded
many notable artists to
provide designs.

THIS POLYCHROME
painted pottery
figure of a young
girl is entitled "Shy"
and was modeled
by Phoebe Stabler.
A sculptor and
designer of some
repute, Phoebe was
married to Harold
Stabler, a director of
Poole Pottery, and
she sold her designs
to several factories.
It is also possible to
find examples of the same
figure produced by Poole Pottery and Royal
Doulton, the only variation
being in the size and material used.

Height 11½in/29cm $C

Ashtead Pottery II

THIS BLUE-GLAZED POTTERY LION WAS DESIGNED by Percy Metcalfe, a well-known sculptor and stamp designer. Originally made for the 1924 Empire Exhibition at Wembley, London, it was called the Lion of Industry. It proved so popular that the "Wembley Lion" was put into general production and adopted by the Genozo toothpaste manufacturer for its advertising.

ALTHOUGH ASHTEAD POTTERY ENJOYED SOME COMMERCIAL success in the 1920s, it was unable to survive the Depression and closed in 1935. Ashtead pieces are clearly marked with the factory name and often carry a painted serial number which refers to the design and the factory order book.

Height 10in/25cm $B

Boch Frères I

*AS WITH SO MANY CONTINENTAL EUROPEAN
potteries, little is known of this Belgian factory, also
called Keramis, because it sustained heavy damage
in World War II and most of its records were
destroyed. What is known is that it was part of
a larger group founded in 1767 at Sept Fontaines in
the Saar region of Germany. In the mid-19th
century, the company split and a new factory was
established at La Louvière in Belgium.*

*BOCH FRÈRES WAS MOST FAMOUS FOR ITS EARTHENWARE
vases, but also had a reputation for using distinctive
decorative techniques and Art Deco shapes and
designs. Its was one of the most important Belgian
contributions to the Art Deco style.*

*THIS VASE REFLECTS THE POPULARITY OF GEOMETRIC
forms, inspired by Cubism and Futurism. Asymmetry
was the new modern look, seeking to escape the
organic style and free-flowing lines of Art Nouveau.*

Height 10in/25cm $C

Boch Frères II

*B*OTH THE SHAPE AND THE DECORATION OF
this vase are typical of Boch Frères, whose distinctive
wares were first incised with the basic pattern and
then covered with a base coating of a thick
crackle glaze in a neutral color. The pot was
then enameled in bold colors within the incised
pattern to create an overall effect that was
reminiscent of Chinese cloisonné.

*A*S IN THE ART NOUVEAU PERIOD, THE DEPICTION OF
the female form was a popular motif in decorative
ceramics. But on this piece the look has been
transformed from romantic notions of womanhood
to a more geometric and abstract style. Factory
marks are usually a variant of "Keramis" or "Boch
Frères," or a combination of the two.

Height 12in/30cm $D

Burleigh 1

*Founded in 1877,
the Burleigh factory
originally specialized
in printed tableware.
During the 1930s,
however, it branched
out into hand-painted
decorative pieces.
Today, the factory is
best known for its
distinctive range of
pitchers with modeled
handles. Production
of this line began in
1931 and continued
until the 1950s.*

*The early models,
often designed by
Charles Wilkes,
had handles
shaped as birds
or animals.
These pitchers,
with parrot
and kingfisher
handles, are typical.
Since the line was
popular and remained
in production for a long
time, examples are still
fairly easy to find and
reasonably inexpensive to buy.*
Height 9in/23cm $A (both)

Burleigh II

Several other lines were produced by Burleigh, but in smaller quantities. One of these featured human figures on the handle. Sports subjects, such as golfers and tennis players, are often found. More unusual was this type of model, depicting the Changing of the Guard at Buckingham Palace, which came in various palettes. The relative rarity of such pitchers means that they tend to command higher prices at auction.

Height 9in/23cm $E

Pre-World War II items commonly carry the factory's distinctive mark, a beehive surrounded by a wreath of leaves.

René Buthaud

Trained in fine art, René Buthaud (1886–1986) turned to ceramics in 1919. He generally worked in stoneware and was one of the chief exponents of sgraffito, a technique that involves dipping a piece of one color into a contrasting slip, then carving away the slip to reveal the color beneath.

Buthaud's other specialty was hand-painted figural decoration – this scene of Europa and the Bull was painted directly on the pot. Buthaud favored blue-gray or iron-red on a stone or cream ground, and his female figures usually have strong outlines. His work, which generally bears his painted signature or initials, is highly collectible, especially in the U.S. and France.

Height 12½in/32cm $G

Carlton Ware 1

BASED IN **S**TOKE-ON-**T**RENT, THE HOME OF
*English pottery, Carlton Ware was a brand name
of Wiltshaw & Robinson. Carlton
produced a wide range of ceramics during
its long history (1890–1992). The output during
the 1920s and '30s included four
distinct areas: molded tablewares; exotic luster ware;
geometric shaped pieces known as the
Moderne line; and those with brightly
colored stylized designs.*

PIECES OF TABLEWARE DECORATED WITH EMBOSSED,
*or relief-molded, flowers, vegetables, and fruit
were a particular specialty of the factory, as were
small and novelty items made out of leaves.
This salad bowl with lobster-claw feet is typical.
It is from the popular Salad Ware line and takes the
form of lettuce leaves with tomatoes.
Since such pieces were made in large numbers, they
are, at present, less collectible than
some of Carlton's other wares.*
Diameter 12in/30cm $A

Carlton Ware II

CARLTON WARE'S LUXURY lines were in direct competition with Wedgwood's Fairyland Lustre and some of Crown Devon's lines. To survive, Carlton endeavored to make quality its byword – and it undoubtedly succeeded. Every piece was hand painted, and many were embellished with gilding, although little is known of the individuals who produced them.

THIS COOKIE JAR, A TYPICAL EXAMPLE, WAS DECORATED with the "Egyptian Fan" design. The pattern is simply one example of the influence that the discovery of Tutankhamun's tomb in 1922 had on popular culture. The name "Egyptian Fan" was one of those given to patterns by recent collectors to help them identify different designs. This was necessary because, although every item was marked on the base with a pattern number, no official names existed.

Height 5½in/14cm $B

Pieces from the Art Deco period usually have a transfer-printed factory mark in script on the base. Any numbers painted alongside the mark denote the serial number of the design.

Carlton Ware III

IN ADDITION TO MAKING TRADITIONAL WARES, *Carlton's designers embraced the modern era, as can be seen in this magnificent "Moderne" tea set, with its attractive matte gray glaze and gilt handles. Legend has it that a French designer sought refuge in England during World War II and briefly worked at the factory, leaving behind this avant-garde shape, but no records exist to confirm the story.*

Height coffee pot 8in/20cm   Set $B

TO THE LEFT OF THE TEA SET ARE TWO OTHER PIECES WITH *the bright-colored, stylized designs typical of Carlton. The pitcher features the "Tiger Tree" design; the ginger jar and cover display the "Sunburst" pattern.*

Height both 8in/20cm $B (jug); $C (jar)

Clarice Cliff 1

One of the dominant designers of the
*Art Deco period, Clarice Cliff (1899–1972) started
out at A.J. Wilkinson's Royal Staffordshire
Pottery in Burslem, where she fell in love with the
factory boss, Colley Shorter. With his guidance, she
underwent a long period of training, which
included regular visits to Paris and London to see
what was at the forefront of modern design.*
In 1927 she was given her own studio and assistants
*at another Wilkinson factory, the Newport
Pottery, and was extremely successful between the
wars. Cliff designed both the shape and decoration of
her wares, which were then hand-copied by her
team. Part of her talent lay in taking
sophisticated avant-garde designs from Europe and
reworking them for the British market.
This single-handled Lotus pitcher is decorated in the
"Blue W" pattern, using the classic colors that
Cliff employed for almost all her designs.*
Height 12in/30cm $G

Clarice Cliff II

Cliff BEGAN HER CAREER WITH SIMPLE GEOMETRIC designs, now commonly known as "Original Bizarre" because the factory mark has the "Bizarre" brand name. Later she progressed to more exciting abstract designs inspired by the French Cubists.

In ADDITION TO GEOMETRIC PATTERNS, SHE DESIGNED lines featuring stylized landscapes. Commercially, they were more successful than the abstract patterns, and many survive. These bright scenes brought cheer to people in the Depression and were favored as wedding presents.

Pieces IN UNUSUAL SHAPES, SUCH AS CONICAL SUGAR sifters, are particularly popular with collectors. This one features a typical landscape design known as "House and Bridge." Behind is a baluster vase in the "Oranges" pattern and to the right a small vase in the "Orange Roof Cottage" design. The beaker in the foreground is decorated with the classic abstract pattern "Tennis."

Height large vase 8½in/22cm $D (all)

Clarice Cliff III

DURING THE EARLY 1930S, Clarice Cliff became involved with the Harrods Exhibition, for which many artists of the day turned their talents to designing tableware. Her studio at Wilkinson's produced the pottery, while the china and glasswares were made elsewhere.

FOLLOWING THE DEATH OF HIS INVALID WIFE, Colley Shorter finally married Cliff in 1940. With a happy marriage and the factory restricted to making utility ware during World War II, Cliff went into semi-retirement, which later became permanent. She has left a legacy of designs which still appeal today.

THE TOP PLATE is decorated in the "Sunray" pattern, which is said to have been inspired by the skyscrapers of New York. Many collectors call this design "Night and Day," after the Cole Porter song. The lower plate features another classic abstract design known as "Lightning."

Diameter both 8in/20cm $D

Clarice Cliff IV

*THE POPULARITY OF CLARICE CLIFF'S WORK
means that fakes abound. Although these two
examples of the "Orange Roof Cottage" pattern
look similar, the pitcher on the right is a fake. It may
seem genuine, but important differences
become obvious when it is next to the original.
The windows of the cottage have reflections;
the bridge is misdrawn; and the color scheme
is wrong: the orange banding in the copy is too bright
and red. (Many of the original, more muted, enamel
colors are toxic and so are now unavailable.)
A convincing factory mark is no guarantee of
authenticity either, since good replicas exist.*
Height left 9in/23cm `$E; right 12in/30cm

Cliff marks are distinctive.
In the years 1929–39, they
were put on in black either
with a rubber stamp or with
a simple lithograph over the
glaze. They usually include
the brand name, such as
"Bizarre," within the mark.

Susie Cooper I

Born in 1902, *Susie Cooper was a contemporary of Clarice Cliff, but outlived her more successful rival. She began her career at A.E. Gray & Co. Ltd. in 1922 and was soon given her own designer backstamp. During her seven years at Gray's, Cooper became involved in luster decoration, only later moving on to more abstract Cubist designs. Of her many different design periods, only the Cubist bears comparison with the work of Clarice Cliff. This vase, decorated with the "Moon and Mountain" pattern, is typical of Cooper's output at that time.*

Height 8in/20cm $D

Susie Cooper's distinctive backstamp while at Gray's consisted of the liner mark of Gray's pottery with the legend "Designed by Susie Cooper" below.

Susie Cooper II

ONE OF SUSIE COOPER'S MOST FAMOUS SHAPES *was that of the "Kestrel" line, introduced at the British Industries Fair in 1932. The distinctive design, shown here in the form of a coffeepot, is set off by the decoration, obviously inspired by the abstract artist Piet Mondrian.*

COOPER EXPERIENCED PROBLEMS WITH HER EARLY *on-glaze decoration, and many examples of her work from this period are in poor repair. She had particular trouble with oxidizing or flaking enamels, a problem Clarice Cliff also encountered but overcame sooner.*

Height 10in/25cm $C (pot)

Susie Cooper III

*I*N 1930 *S*USIE *C*OOPER *BEGAN DESIGNING AND
*producing her own wares. One of her independent
ventures was at Wood & Son's Crown Works in
Burslem, in The Potteries. This animal plate – typical
of her output at the time – has been delicately hand-
painted in the center and enhanced with silver
luster. It also shows one of Cooper's favorite later
techniques,* sgraffito *decoration, around the rim.*

Diameter 8in/20cm $D

*S*USIE *C*OOPER *WAS AT THE FOREFRONT OF *M*ODERNISM
*and favored modern industrial techniques to
produce tableware that was easy to use and maintain.
In later years, she took up the new lithographed
decorative techniques suitable for mass production.
After a long and varied career, she went to work
for Wedgwood after World War II.*

Susie Cooper IV

TOWARD THE END OF THE ART DECO PERIOD,
Susie Cooper produced a line of studio wares with a
more handmade feel. This example, which is signed,
is from the "Carved Ware" line, which features
simple forms incised with animal designs.
Height 12in/30cm $B

Susie Cooper's
later pieces bear
her distinctive flowing
signature incised
on the base.

Crown Devon I

Like Carlton Ware, Crown Devon produced a full range of table and fancy wares, and was based near Stoke-on-Trent. Indeed, the two firms were direct rivals, and many of their goods, in particular the luster wares, are virtually indistinguishable. This can be explained by the fact that two of the leading lights at Carlton, Enoch Wood and George Barker, defected to Crown Devon in 1930 as decorating manager and sales director respectively.

This vase is typical of Crown Devon's luster-decorated pieces. The glossy blue ground is enameled in colors and gilt with an outlandish floral pattern.

Height 6¾in/17cm **$B**

Crown Devon
is clearly printed
"Fielding's,"
representing S. Fielding
& Co., of which
Crown Devon was
the brand name.

Crown Devon II

THE CROSS-FERTILIZATION OF IDEAS BETWEEN
*Carlton and Crown Devon was not unusual in this
period: market share was vital at a time of limited
sales, and companies regularly took good ideas from
various sources and developed them further. Crown
Devon competed in the market for Goldscheider- and
Katzhütte-type pottery figures, for example,
ruthlessly copying successful models.*

THIS VASE FROM THE MATTE-DECORATED LINE SHOWS
*strong enamel color and delicate gilding. The
spider's web was a popular motif in the Art Deco
period because of its strong geometric qualities.*

Height 6¾in/17cm $B

French porcelain 1

In Europe, one of the more popular Art Deco figural pieces was the luminaire, *or night light, which provided the subtle lighting considered essential for creating the right atmosphere in the home. Since porcelain becomes translucent when fired, it is perfect for night lights – no other ceramic material allows light to filter through.*

Many night-light shapes were inspired by the popular culture of the day. This typical example by Delblaize depicts Harlequin and Columbine from the Commedia dell'Arte plays. Nothing is known of the artist, who simply signed his name on the piece. This is not an uncommon phenomenon, since factories often sold undecorated items to artists and then re-fired the painted articles in their kiln.

Height 11in/28cm $D

French porcelain II

FOLLOWING A TRADITION OF ABOUT 200 YEARS
*of manufacture by such leading factories as Sèvres
and Limoges, French Art Deco porcelain
was among the highest quality. These exquisitely
decorated plates are part of a service of 18, each
signed "G. Nielz, Delveaux." No information exists
on either artist or manufacturer – Delveaux may
have have been the retailer's mark or the trade
name for a larger manufacturer.*

MADE FOR THE LUXURY END OF THE MARKET, EACH PLATE
*is painted in brilliant colors, both under and over
the glaze. The subject, scenes of marine life, was
popular in France at the time, since biologist Jacques
Cousteau had recently invented the aqualung,
furthering study of life under the sea.*

Diameter 8in/20cm $E

German pottery

ALTHOUGH GERMANY produced some first-class porcelain and was famous for factories such as Rosenthal and Meissen, stoneware and pottery were favored at the more popular end of the market because they tended to be less expensive to produce.

THIS POTTERY PIECE is typical of German figural works of the period. They almost always feature young women in evening gowns or other slightly risqué clothing, often leading a terrier or exotic borzoi hound. This model is wearing a sunsuit with lounging pyjamas – then the height of fashion. Since the piece was made for export, the base is simply marked "Germany."

Height 9½in/24cm   \$C

German stoneware

THIS STONEWARE GROUP, BASED ON GREEK MYTH, depicts Neptune, rather improbably dressed in what looks like a fireman's helmet and waterproof trousers, astride a hippocampus, or sea horse.
THE HEAVY CRACKLED GLAZE HAS BEEN SUBTLY PAINTED IN shades of blue and green, and given a second firing. Unlike the figure opposite, which was mass-produced, this piece – with its high-quality composition and execution – was almost certainly the work of an artist: the absence of a factory mark suggests that it came from a small studio working either within a larger factory or independently.
Height 14in/36cm $E

Ginori

ORIGINALLY KNOWN AS THE DOCCIA FACTORY, *Ginori was founded near Florence in 1737 by Carlo Ginori, who brought the secret of porcelain manufacture from Vienna. During the late 19th century, it was adapted for mass production, and in 1896 it amalgamated with another factory to become Richard-Ginori, although it is now commonly known simply as Ginori.*

BETWEEN 1923 AND 1938, IT EMPLOYED THE NOW-FAMOUS *Italian architect and designer Gio Ponti to revitalize its output. Although he was avant-garde, he also liked to rework traditional shapes and motifs. This porcelain box and cover decorated with silver luster, entitled "Balletto," is typical of his work. The stylized figures are mounted on a conventional fluted oval form decorated with sprays of foliage.*

Height 9in/23cm $F

Goldscheider 1

ONE OF THE LARGEST
*Austrian ceramics manufacturers of the Art Deco
era, the Goldscheider factory had a thriving export
business. Polychrome pottery figures, often designed
by outside artists, formed much of its output.
They tend to be fragile and may crack at weaker
points such as the wrists and ankles.*

THE LEFT AND CENTRAL FIGURES HERE ARE BY THE AUSTRIAN
*sculptor Stefan Dakon, who also worked in
bronze and ivory. These hand-painted pieces bear
Dakon's signature as well as the factory mark. The
piece on the right is unsigned, but is typical of Josef
Lorenzl, who also often worked for the firm.*
Height left 4⅓in/11cm $E (center); $D (others)

Goldscheider II

DURING THE **A**RT **D**ECO period, Goldscheider also specialized in terracotta wall masks. With their stylized lines and primary colors, they owe much to the work of the Austrian Modernist group, the Wiener Werkstätte. Only a few models were made, but they were hand painted in numerous color schemes.

SINCE TERRACOTTA IS delicate, porous, and easily damaged, examples in perfect condition are now rare. The coiled hair tends to crack first.

FROM THE LATE 1930S, GOLDSCHEIDER PIECES WERE made in Staffordshire by Myott, Son & Co. Similar masks were also made in central Europe, although those made there since 1945 are easy to identify – they are marked only with their country of origin and tend to be less well made.

Height 11in/28cm   \$C

Goldscheider wares have a thick crackled glaze and distinctive factory mark. Earlier models were often marked "Wien" (Vienna), while later models made for export were marked "Made in Austria."

Carruthers Gould

PRODUCED AT THE **W**ILKINSON FACTORY,
*these pottery Toby jugs were based on designs by
the famous political cartoonist Sir Francis
Carruthers Gould (1844–1920). Although not Art
Deco in the strict sense of the word, they are typical
of the patriotic commemorative pieces produced
in Britain between the wars and
depict figures such as Lloyd George and Lord
Kitchener. Commemorative wares celebrating Allied
successes in World War I were vital in boosting
morale during the Depression.*
Height 10in/25cm $G

Geneviève Granger

ONE OF THE FEW COMMERCIALLY SUCCESSFUL
*female sculptors of the time, this French-born artist
produced works in terracotta, bronze, ivory,
and pottery. She was well known and showed at the
Paris Exhibition of 1925 – commonly seen as
heralding the start of the Art Deco period.*
MOST OF HER MODELS WERE FIRST MADE IN BRONZE AT THE
*Etling foundry and only then passed to the ceramics
manufacturer. They usually carry a triangular
impressed factory mark, "Editions Etling," and a
facsimile signature. This pottery model of a naked
woman, with its simple lines and low-key decoration,
is typical of her work. It has a crackle glaze with
blue sponged painting to the head and base.*
Height 15in/38cm $D

Gustavsberg

Dᴜʀɪɴɢ ᴛʜᴇ Aʀᴛ Dᴇᴄᴏ ᴘᴇʀɪᴏᴅ, Gᴜsᴛᴀᴠsʙᴇʀɢ,
one of Sweden's oldest ceramics factories, was at
the forefront of Scandinavian Modernism. The
driving force behind the factory was its
artistic director, Wilhem Kåge, who worked
there between 1917 and 1950.

"Aʀɢᴇɴᴛᴀ" ᴡᴀʀᴇ, ɪɴᴛʀᴏᴅᴜᴄᴇᴅ ʙʏ Kåɢᴇ ɪɴ 1930, ᴡᴀs
one of Gustavsberg's most famous lines.
Usually glazed in matte green or a deep mottled
burgundy, it had rich silver inlay. This charger is
decorated with mermaids, a motif popular then, and
the glaze has been applied to simulate bubbles.
Pieces from the line are usually fully marked in
silver and carry the pattern number.

Diameter 18in/46cm $D

Harrods Exhibition I

HELD AT
London's famous
department store in 1934,
the Harrods Exhibition was
the brainchild of painter Graham Sutherland, designer
Milner Gray, and manufacturer Thomas Acland
Fennemore, director of E. Brain & Co. Its purpose
was to produce a series of designs, both on
ceramics and on glass, which would show that it was
possible to unite artists and industry, and make
modern art accessible to the average person.
A LEADING LIGHT OF THE BLOOMSBURY GROUP, VANESSA BELL
(1879–1961) was one of 28 artists and designers
invited to submit ideas for tableware. These pieces
are from a complete dinner service, entitled
"Vanessa," produced in Clarice Cliff's workshop at
Wilkinson's. Each one was painted freehand in blue
enamel on an opaque white glaze and has a
band of brown dots around the rim.
Diameter plates 8in/20cm $E–$G

Harrods Exhibition II

THREE SITES WERE USED FOR PRODUCING EXHIBITION *wares: A.J. Wilkinson's for the pottery; E. Brain & Co. (also known as Foley China) for the bone china; and Stuart Glass. Just 12 services were made of each design and were marked "First edition" on the reverse; the most popular later went into large-scale production. Many of the designs submitted were unsuitable – they were impractical either as tableware or for mass production. But enough exhibition ware exists today to make it a worthwhile collecting field in its own right.*

DAME LAURA KNIGHT (1877–1970) WAS ONE OF *the most commercially successful British artists of the era and contributed several designs to the exhibition. This tea service, entitled "Cupid," was made at Foley China. Its printed outline is enameled in black and green. Since the black enamel tends to lift and flake off, care must be taken when handling pieces.*

Height cup 1½in/4cm $D–$F

Harrods Exhibition III

IMAGES OF CIRCUS LIFE WERE A favored motif for Laura Knight. Her "Circus" series, produced by Clarice Cliff at Wilkinson's, is the best known and most sought after today. Part of its popularity may be due to the fact that Knight, unlike the other artists, also designed the shapes for her extensive service. All the items, from tureens to pitchers and bowls, had finials and legs modeled as intertwined clowns.

THIS TABLE LAMP, ONE OF ONLY three known to exist, matches the rest of the service and represents the apogee of the style. The column of intertwined circus folk is enameled in bright colors embellished with gilt. The top is painted with swags reminiscent of the top of a tent – a motif repeated across the service, especially as an edging on plates. An underglaze pink transfer print was the starting point for applying the decoration, which was then enameled free-hand on glaze.

Height 19in/48cm $G

Harrods Exhibition IV

THIS PLATE WAS ONE OF THE FOLEY-PRODUCED
line of Laura Knight designs. The whole pattern is
painted freehand in colors and purple luster, and
appears to represent Adam and Eve in the Garden of
Eden, although the exact title is unknown. The
theme does, however, fit in with another of
Knight's patterns for Foley, which is entitled "Dove"
and depicts scenes after the Flood.

PERHAPS BECAUSE THE COMPOSITION IS RELATIVELY
weak and the luster prone to wear, this was the least
produced of Laura Knight's designs, and
examples of it are hardest to find.

Diameter 8in/20cm $D

Harrods Exhibition v

THIS HIGHLY SUCCESSFUL PATTERN BY
Ernest Proctor (1885–1935) was produced at
Wilkinson's on green-glazed pottery. It was painted
freehand in silver luster in Clarice Cliff's studio.
Proctor's wife Dod also designed for the exhibition.
Diameter 8in/20cm $B

IT IS NOT KNOWN HOW MANY EXHIBITION DESIGNS
were put into production, but each piece is clearly
marked on the reverse with a printed factory
backstamp and the artist's signature. In addition to
the artists featured here, others whose work was
produced include John Armstrong, Freda Beardmore,
Angelica Bell, Frank Brangwyn, Eva Crofts, John
Everett, Gordon Forsyth, Moira Forsyth, Duncan
Grant, Milner Gray, Barbara Hepworth, Paul Nash,
Ben Nicholson, Albert Rutherston, Graham
Sutherland, Allan Walton, and Michael Wellmer.

Harrods Exhibition VI

BILLY WATERS (1896–1979) SPENT FIVE YEARS AT
*Newlyn, Cornwall, where she studied under Ernest
Proctor. Today she is best known for the quality
of her designs. This soup bowl and stand are part of
a dinner service produced at Wilkinson's.
Printed and painted in grays, greens, and blacks on
pottery, this highly successful design could be easily
adapted for tableware shapes and lent itself to
industrial production. The service is even durable
enough to withstand modern use.*
THE LEAPING DEER IS A COMMON MOTIF ON 1930s DESIGNS.
*Susie Cooper used it on her factory backstamp when
her studio was at the Crown Works, Burslem. It
was also used at Poole Pottery, incorporated into
delicately scrolling foliage, where it proved so
successful that the design is still in production today.*
Diameter bowl 4¼in/11cm $B

Katzhütte Thuringia

DECORATIVE EARTHENWARE figures produced for the lower end of the market were the specialty of this small factory. Thuringia, one of the centers of the German ceramics industry, played host to many small factories, much like Limoges in France.

KATZHÜTTE'S CHARMING figures capture the spirit of the day. They often feature movie stars, since this was the age when films first caught the public imagination. There are also sports subjects, since in prewar Germany, it was considered both fashionable and beneficial to be healthy.

THIS FIGURE OF A DANCING LADY IN A BIAS-CUT GOWN AND large hat is typical of Katzhütte's output.

Height 14in/36cm $C

The highly distinctive factory mark takes the form of a pictogram. Katzhütte literally means "cat's house," so the mark shows a cat, with the letter H above it, inside a house.

Robert Lallement

A WELL-KNOWN FRENCH CERAMICS DESIGNER,
Robert Lallement (1902–54) caught the flavor of
the Art Deco period. After initial training at
Lachenal, a large pottery manufacturer in Paris, he
set up his own small enterprise in that city.
*T*HE MAJORITY OF HIS PIECES ARE SIMPLE GEOMETRIC FORMS,
usually vases, on which his own designs are
painted. These examples are typical: the square vase
on the left is painted with scenes of Chopin
playing to an attentive audience; on the right is a
bowed rectangular vase painted with the popular
Art Deco motif of a browsing deer. Although the
pottery itself is quite fragile, the decoration is
applied with assurance and style. Most
pieces are signed in black with "Lallement"
in capital letters or script.
Height left 8in/20cm $D; right 5in/13cm $C

Lenci 1

*Established in Turin in 1919, the Lenci factory
was at the forefront of Italian Art Deco. Its output
was considerable and included much that catered for
the religious tastes of the home market,
such as Madonna and Child groups and wall masks
of modest ladies. Although best known for its figures,
Lenci also made decorative tableware which, until
1939, was painted with Cubist designs.*

*This group, entitled "Mamma Sirena," was designed
in 1935 by Helen König Scavini, one of Lenci's top
designers. It is a fantasy representation of
motherhood – a common theme – and uses matte
and shiny glazes, a feature of many Lenci pieces.*

Height 14in/36cm $G

Lenci II

THIS SHINY-GLAZED *Betty Grable-style figure, attributed to Lenci, was designed by an unknown artist. Such figures of immodestly dressed women were popular with the designers, but did not sell in large numbers and are now hard to find, although they are favored by today's collectors.* **IN THE 1930s,** *figures of women in contemporary fashion were preferred to nudes.*

Height 13in/33cm **SE**

Lenci factory marks are usually hand painted in black on the base. They are often dated and sometimes carry an artist's insignia, although many designers remained anonymous. The "Made in Italy" mark shows that this piece was destined for export. Occasionally, it is possible to find a piece's original paper label.

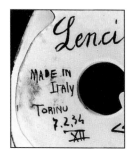

Limoges

FINE CERAMICS HAVE BEEN MADE IN the city of Limoges, France, since the 17th century, but it is only since the 1870s that they have been mass produced. As in Thuringia, Germany, many small companies traded under the Limoges name, among them Serpaut, which made this piece.

PORCELAIN NIGHT lights such as this were essential in the 1920s and '30s home. The Egyptian style, sparked by the discovery of Tutankhamun's tomb in 1922, is evident in the design of a high priestess holding sacrificial bowls. Priestesses were a popular motif and can be seen in much of the decorative art of the period.

Height 6¾in/17cm $C

The Limoges mark from this period is quite distinctive. In addition to the mark shown here, pieces usually carried pattern and factory names.

Longwy

THE CERAMICISTS AT THE FRENCH FACTORY LONGWY
used the same technique as Boch Frères to make this
pottery plate. The cloisonné effect, which imitates
Persian patterns, was developed in the Bordeaux
region by artists such as Theodor Deck, but became
popular with many manufacturers.
MADE FOR THE FRENCH DESIGN STUDIO PRIMAVERA, PART OF
the Paris department store Au Printemps, this piece
has enameled decoration and features a jungle
landscape with naked women. It was inspired
by the recent interest of artists such as Picasso in
African art. The piece is stamped "Primavera
Longwy France" on the base.

Diameter 14½in/37cm $E

Moorcroft

WILLIAM MOORCROFT (1872–1945) LEARNED HIS
*trade at James Macintyre & Co. in Staffordshire
before setting up his own company in 1913. The
pottery is distinctive because the outlines of
the designs – commonly flowers, fungi, or landscapes –
are made using a kind of tube-lining technique.
This magnificent vase, dated 1928, is decorated with
a combination of two well-known patterns,
"Eventide" and "Moonlit Blue."*
IT IS MARKED WITH AN IMPRESSED "MOORCROFT" AND THE
*painted initials "W.M.," which between the wars
were generally blue. The factory remains in family
hands and is still true to its founder's style.*
Height 18½in/47cm $G

Keith Murray

THIS NEW ZEALAND-BORN DESIGNER
(1892–1981) worked on a freelance
basis at Wedgwood from 1933 to
1946 while waiting to find a
suitable position in his chosen
profession of architecture.
He designed a series
of pots and
tableware
which had a
great impact.
His style was
a precursor of
the fashion for
simplicity which informed British design
after 1945, and his shapes were produced at
Wedgwood into the 1950s.

MURRAY'S DESIGNS WERE MADE EITHER IN
earthenware or in the black and brown basalt for
which Wedgwood is famous. Often they were
molded, but the basalt pieces at the top of the line
had linear decoration carved in the body.
The earthenware pieces were covered in matte
colored glazes designed for the
line. The black basalt wares – signed on
the bottom in red – are his rarest.

Diameter vase 10in/25cm $B; $D (bowl)

Prewar pieces are easily
identified by the full printed
signature, like this one, in the
backstamp. It is usually beneath
the glaze and can be any color.
Items made after 1941 were
simply marked "K.M."

Keith Murray
WEDGWOOD
MADE IN ENGLAND

Poole Pottery I

Founded in the 1870s as a tile manufacturer,
Poole Pottery became a partnership between the
original owner Cyril Carter, John Adams, and Harold
Stabler; it was finally named after the Dorset
town where it is still based. Adams was responsible
for new shapes and glazes, while Carter's wife
Truda designed the patterns, and Phoebe and
Harold Stabler the sculptural pieces.
This impressive vase, made between 1929 and 1934,
was designed by Truda Carter and decorated by Ann
Hatchard, a senior painter. Its black ground
is unusual, but its dense stylized foliage is typical.
Height 19in/48cm $G

Poole Pottery II

POOLE POTTERY WARE IS TYPIFIED BY A CREAMY *crackle glaze over red earthenware pottery, which was painted in muted pastel shades with dense floral, animal, and bird designs. After a while, the source for the red earthenware dried up, but the company continued with ordinary white pottery, dipped in red slip, which was covered in a cream or gray crackle glaze. This is why a distinctive ring is often found on the base of the pot: when the factory mark was impressed into the clay, it left a ring of white around the central mark.*

THIS PLATE IS DECORATED WITH A DESIGN BY TRUDA CARTER, *adapted from a Harold Stabler faience panel design. The design was converted to a mosaic floor for the 1928 Building Trades Exhibition.*

Diameter 16in/40cm $D

Charlotte Rhead 1

*CHARLOTTE RHEAD (1885–1947) WAS THE THIRD
generation of a family of Staffordshire potters. These
pieces are typical of her work – pottery with
tube-lining decoration. The pitcher at the back is in
the "Palermo" pattern, produced from c.1932
and one of her more Art Deco style designs. Of the
other pieces, only those center back and bottom
right have a pattern name – "Wisteria."*
Height "Palermo" pitcher 8in/20cm $B (all)

Charlotte Rhead II

*THIS PLAQUE IS POSSIBLY THE RAREST EXAMPLE OF
Charlotte Rhead's work known. It is a reworking
of one of the earliest patterns that she produced, in
1915 when she was working for Wood & Sons,
and shows Japanese scenes, which had become
popular in the Art Nouveau period and remained
so until the outbreak of World War II.*

Diameter 12in/30cm $G

Charlotte Rhead often
wrote the "C" of her
signature as an "L" with
a long underline
since she preferred
to be known as Lottie.
The number is that
of the pattern.

Rosenthal

Founded in 1879 in Bavaria, the Rosenthal factory established itself before the end of the century, producing high-quality bone china tableware in the Art Nouveau style. The factory remained at the forefront of current styles and even today collaborates with contemporary artists to produce lithographed limited edition plates.

In the 1920s and '30s, it made many Art Deco figures and groups in porcelain, with either a pale cream or clear glaze. This bust, with its stylized form and angular lines, is typical. Factory marks are usually underglaze transfer printed in green, and the incised artist's insignia is often on the body.

Height 19in/48cm $D

Royal Copenhagen

Established in 1873, this factory is the major ceramics producer in Denmark and is endorsed by the Danish royal family. Today it is well known for its reproductions of old tableware patterns and for its porcelain figurines, painted in shades of mushroom and blue.

This distinctive gray stoneware figure, with its mottled brown glaze, is a departure from the factory's standard work and was one of a group of stoneware figures, mostly of animal subjects. It was originally modeled in the early 1930s and was probably designed by Knud Khyn (1880–1969), who was responsible for the series.

It represents Harvest, with a nude woman standing in front of sheaves of wheat. All Royal Copenhagen ceramics are clearly marked in underglaze blue, usually with three wavy lines and the serial number of the model.

Height 19¼in/49cm $C

Royal Doulton 1

Founded in 1815, Royal Doulton has been making figurines since c.1913, and in that time, more than 2,000 models have appeared. One of the best-known figurine designers was Leslie Harradine (1887–1965). In the late 1920s, he made several figures of flappers, bathers, and so forth. Most of these were in production for only a short period because they were deemed too risqué. Figure H.N. 1204, made from 1925 to 1940, is typical, with her vaudeville performer's dress and fan. Originally called "Fanny," she was renamed "Angela," but even this more decorous name did not keep her in production.

Height 7¼in/18.5cm $D

Royal Doulton figures are usually catalogued by their "H.N." number, referring to Harry Nixon, who was largely responsible for starting the figurine line. Originally they had a printed factory mark with the name and H.N. number painted, usually in green or black, but now the whole mark is printed.

Royal Doulton II

"CHORUS GIRL," H.N. 1401, WAS ONE OF the many figurines modeled by Leslie Harradine and was produced from 1930 to 1936. Originally launched in 1923 as "Harlequinade," a slightly more demure model, she was intended to depict Columbine from the Commedia dell'Arte plays and was one of Royal Doulton's first ladies to sport the new shorter-length dress. "Harlequinade" was taken out of production shortly after the introduction of "Chorus Girl."

Height 8½in/21.5cm $D

"THE PRINCE OF WALES," H.N. 1217, AGAIN modeled by Harradine, was produced from 1926 to 1938. This time, it was not deference to social mores that caused the figure to be withdrawn, but Edward VIII's abdication to marry Wallis Simpson in 1936. Based on a portrait by Sir Alfred Munnings, it was sold for two years after the abdication, perhaps because Edward was still so popular.

Height 7¼in/18.5cm $D

"BILLY BUNNIKINS" COMES FROM A SERIES OF nursery ware designed in the 1930s by Barbara Vernon, also known as Sister Mary Barbara, daughter of the general manager of Doulton's at the time. The original Bunnikins figures (six in all) were produced for only a few years from 1938 and were withdrawn in World War II.

Height 4in/10cm $D

Sèvres 1

The French factory Sèvres is most famous for its 18th-century porcelain. But the Art Deco pieces produced in the 1920s and '30s, when Sèvres had the best-known contemporary artists and designers working for it, are also exquisite.

Designed by Jacques-Emile Ruhlmann (1879–1933), this bronze-mounted porcelain vase was decorated by Adrien-August Leduc. Ruhlmann, one of the foremost exponents of the Art Deco style, is best known for his furniture. The subtlety of this abstract design is typical of the period, but its superb quality could only be by Sèvres. The vase is signed "A. Leduc" and is dated 1931. It also bears a paper label inscribed "18-2 2.050-Ruhlmann-Leduc."

Height 8½in/22cm $G

Sèvres II

JEAN MAYODON (1893–1967) *worked for many years at the Sèvres factory and eventually became its artistic director in 1941–42. Among his artistic endeavors are several important commissions for the luxury liner* S.S. Normandie, *launched in 1935 and famous for its interior decor in the Art Deco style.* **MAYODON WAS A KEEN** *experimentalist in glazing and firing techniques, as can be seen on this vase, which is decorated with the "net of gold" technique for which he is best known. He is also identified with classical Greek subject matter, evidenced by this composition of mythological figures. In this instance, the base is marked with the artist's monogram, although not all of his works are signed.*

Height 12in/30cm $G

Shelley I

THE SHELLEY WORKS (1910–66) DEVELOPED FROM the Staffordshire company Foley Wileman, founded in the late 19th century. Although best known for its Art Deco bone china tea sets, Shelley extended the line into dinner services, the larger pieces of which were made of a more durable heat-resistant ceramic than that used for cups and saucers.

FROM THE "VOGUE" LINE, THIS SELECTION OF DINNER WARE uses an overlapping rectangle motif, simply printed and enameled in black and orange, and is typical of patterns of this period.

Width platter 15in/38cm   Service $D

THE FACTORY MARK, REGISTERED IN 1910, IS A SIMPLE SHIELD enclosing the word "Shelley." The painted serial numbers accompanying the factory mark refer to the date when the design was introduced, and the letter prefixing the number refers to the cup shape.

Shelley II

THIS CERAMIC MODEL, typically dressed in the clothes of the era, right down to the cloche hat, is the famous "Shelley Girl" designed in the mid-1920s purely for advertising purposes. Intended for use in store displays, she was part of a concerted advertising campaign, which included posters and magazines, to persuade the public that tea drinking was sophisticated and fashionable.

ALTHOUGH SHE BEGAN LIFE without a name, she came to be called Elsie Harding when the company had to invent a character for her because she was so well known. At one point, painters from the factory were given the same style distinctive paisley-patterned dress to wear when they were doing demonstrations in department stores. But Elsie Harding's fame was short-lived, and she disappeared from the advertising campaigns in 1930.

Height 10in/25cm $D

Shelley III

THESE TRIOS OF CUP, saucer, and plate show three of the best-known shapes used in the bone china tea services of the Art Deco era. In most instances, the teapot was an optional extra which was not sold as part of the service.

"VOGUE" (TOP) WAS designed by Shelley's foremost designer, Eric Slater, and introduced in 1930. It is very modern, but the cup is difficult to hold because the triangular handle is solid.

"REGENT" (CENTER) WAS introduced in 1932 and proved to be enduringly popular, perhaps because the form, while stylish, was not too extreme and was also functional.

THE SLIGHTLY OLDER "Queen Anne" style (bottom) came onto the market in 1926. All the trios have small plates in the "Queen Anne" shape.

Width plates 4½in/11.5cm **$A**

John Skeaping

ACTIVE AS A SCULPTOR IN ENGLAND IN THE 1920s and '30s, Skeaping (1901–80) designed a series of animal figures for Wedgwood, for which he was paid a total of £100. At the time, the effects of the Depression were reducing the factory's profits, so it was trying to move away from exclusive high-quality wares toward simpler, less costly designs.

SKEAPING DESIGNED 14 ANIMAL STUDIES, 10 OF WHICH went into mass production. The figures were made in various bodies and glazes, including basalt. This is the "Polar Bear" model, covered in "Moonstone" glaze. The other production models were: "Buffalo," "Tiger and Buck," "Duiker" (a type of antelope) standing and sitting, "Fallow Deer," "Monkeys," "Sea Lion," "Bison," and "Kangaroo." They usually have an impressed signature on the top of the base, but it can be hard to see if the glaze is thick.

Height 7in/18cm $B

Vi.Bi.

THIS SMALL FACTORY IS NOT STRICTLY ART DECO
*because it was founded just after World War II, but
it is included because it shows how the style
endured. Like Lenci, Vi.Bi. was based in Turin, and it
was directly inspired by that company's designs.
It sought to perpetuate the fantasy models
popular before the war, and this example is typical.
Entitled "La Donna e la Piovra," it depicts a woman
trying to escape an amorous octopus. The quality
of the modeling is not quite up to Lenci standards,
so the piece veers toward the kitsch.*

Height 13½in/34cm $G

Wade

THE WADE GROUP WAS FOR MANY years a conglomeration of several small factories trading under the Wade family name, and did not unite as one company until the 1950s. George Wade & Sons was formed in 1867, and between 1927 and 1937 it produced a series of 63 Art Deco pottery figurines and wall masks, designed by Jessica Van Hallen, which are unique in their use of a cellulose finish. The models were fired, then dipped in cellulose and, when dry, painted in colors. Since the colors were not fired onto the body, they often flaked off, and the cellulose itself deteriorated quickly and discolored. Because of this, it is extremely unusual to find examples, such as this figure entitled "Springtime," which are in good condition.

Height 8in/20cm $B

Wade's factory marks are printed on the base with a simple ink stamp. "Wade" is in black, and the leaping deer motif is red.

Louis Wain 1

THE ENGLISH ARTIST AND ILLUSTRATOR LOUIS WAIN
*(1860–1939) spent his life producing comic pictures
of cats and was a household name. In 1914 he began
work on a series of cat mascots, including this version
of the "Lucky Mascot Cat." The musical-style
motifs on the body are "Meow Meow" notes and
appear on several models. Although its whisker is
broken, it is still highly prized and a collector's item.*

Height 11in/28cm $G

AMONG THE OTHER KNOWN FIGURES ARE THE "LUCKY MASTER
*Cat," "Lucky Knight-Errant Cat," and "Lucky
Futurist Cat." They all have an impressed signature on
the body and a cat's paw printed on the base.*

Louis Wain II

OF ALL OF WAIN'S MODELS, THESE ARE PERHAPS THE
most common. Top left is the "Lucky Haw-Haw
Cat," its monocle and cigar identifying it with Lord
Haw-Haw, who later made propaganda broadcasts
for Germany during World War II. The top right
model is unnamed; the one bottom left is the "Lucky
Pig"; that on the right the "Lucky Bully Bulldog."
Height 3½–4½in/9–11.5cm $D (all)

Wedgwood 1

Fairyland Lustre is synonymous with designer Daisy Makeig-Jones (1881–1945), who worked for Wedgwood from 1909 to 1931, producing numerous patterns incorporating fairies, elves, and goblins. The designs were applied to porcelain pieces through a complicated – and not always successful – process of transfer printing, underglaze painting, overglaze luster, and printed gilding.

The "Bubbles II" design on this ginger jar (or Malfrey pot) shows the story of a nix, or waterman. He guarded the souls of the dead in an underwater palace, but a peasant released them all – shown here as black elves escaping in bubbles.

Height 9in/23cm $G

Wedgwood II

*B*EFORE FINALLY CONCENTRATING ON PATTERNS OF
fairies and elves, Daisy Makeig-Jones produced other
fantasy designs. This pair of Dragon Lustre vases
copies 18th-century Chinese porcelain. They date
from the early 1920s and are one of her first designs.
Height 10¼in/26cm $C

The factory mark
is the famous Wedgwood
Portland Vase mark printed
in gilt on the base. On some
of her more elaborate
pieces, Daisy Makeig-Jones
was known to include her
monogram in the
final gilding.

Wiener Werkstätte

FOUNDED BY JOSEF Hoffmann, Koloman Moser, and Fritz Wärndorfer in Vienna, this association of workshops for artists and designers is seen as one of the great Modernist movements of the 20th century, guiding Europe away from Art Nouveau and toward Art Deco. It specialized in unique one-off designs, but was never successful commercially, even though examples can command thousands of dollars at auction and are on show in every major museum worldwide. Although the Wiener Werkstätte was active as early as 1903 – the Art Nouveau period – the earlier pieces looked forward to Art Deco, and many typically Art Deco items were produced until 1932.

THIS TIN-GLAZED RED TERRACOTTA GROUP IS TYPICAL. IT WAS designed by Susi Singer (1881–1965) in the 1920s, when the workshops were under the artistic directorship of Dagobert Pêche who encouraged less severe and more commercially appealing designs. The base is marked with the impressed entwined "W" mark, and with Singer's monogram.

Height 9in/23cm $F

Frank Lloyd Wright

LIKE THE ARTISTS OF THE WIENER WERKSTÄTTE,
Frank Lloyd Wright (1869–1959), the American-
born architect and designer, was a Modernist,
although ironically he was committed to the ideals of
the Arts and Crafts Movement of 19th-century
Britain. His buildings, with their innovative use
of space and light, are considered some of the most
radical and avant-garde of their day.
IN ADDITION TO DESIGNING THE BUILDINGS, WRIGHT
was also responsible for the furniture and fixtures
placed inside them. This service was produced
by the local porcelain firm Noritake for
Tokyo's Imperial Hotel which Wright designed in
1915. The pattern dates from c.1922 and is printed
and enameled in colors, yet it is so modern
that it could easily be mistaken for a piece
of contemporary design.
Diameter largest plate 8in/20cm SE

Glossary

BASALT A fine hard black stoneware made by several of the Staffordshire potteries.

BONE CHINA A type of hard-paste porcelain made from a mixture of bone ash and kaolin.

CRACKLE A network of fine lines or cracks in the glaze caused when the body and the glaze contract at different rates when fired.

EARTHENWARE Porous pottery fired at *c.*900–1,500°F (500–800°C). It must be glazed to be waterproof.

ENAMEL Form of decoration made from a mixture of powdered glass and pigmented metal oxides suspended in an oily medium. The oil burns off during firing, leaving a smooth finish.

FAIENCE French tin-glazed earthenware.

LUSTER WARE Ceramics with a metallic or iridescent finish created by applying a metal oxide to the glaze and firing it in a reduced atmosphere, which converts the oxide back into a metal.

OVERGLAZE DECORATION Enamel colors painted or transfer-printed onto a piece over the glaze and then refired at a relatively low temperature. Also known as on-glaze decoration.

PORCELAIN True, or hard-paste, porcelain is made from china clay and china stone and is white, translucent, strong, and heat-resistant.

POTTERY Another name for earthenware or stoneware.

THE POTTERIES Area in Staffordshire, England, around the towns of Stoke-on-Trent, Burslem, Hanley, Tunstall, Longton, and Fenton where many ceramics factories were based.

SGRAFFITO Design effect created by scratching the surface of a piece or scoring through unfired slip that has been applied to it.

SLIP Liquid clay used as a finish or for decoration.

STONEWARE A hard, dense, non-porous material made from clay fired to a point at which the individual grains of the clay fuse together.

TERRACOTTA Literally "baked earth," this low-fired unglazed earthenware is often rich in iron, so it turns a brick-red color when fired.

TIN GLAZE An opaque white glaze made from the basic lead glaze mixed with tin oxide.

TRANSFER PRINTING Method of applying decoration. A paper print of the design in metallic oxides is wrapped around the piece and burns off when fired.

TUBE LINING Decoration made by piping or trailing thick slip on the surface of a piece.

UNDERGLAZE DECORATION Design applied to a piece before glazing and firing.

Index

A

Adams, John 56
America 77
Armstrong, John 46
Art Nouveau 7, 14, 15,
    59, 60, 76
Arts and Crafts
    Movement 77
Ashtead Pottery 12–13
Au Printemps 53
Austria 37, 38

B

Barker, George 30
basalt 55, 69
Bavaria 60
Beardmore, Freda 46
Belgium 14
Bell, Angelica 46
Bell, Vanessa 42
Bizarre brand 23
Bloomsbury Group 42
Boch Frères 14–15, 53
bone china 43, 60, 66, 68
Bordeaux 53
Brain & Co.,E. 42, 43, 45
Brangwyn, Frank 46
Burleigh 16–17
Burslem 22, 28
Buthaud, René 18

C

Carlton Ware 19–21, 30,
    31
Carter, Cyril 56
Carter, Truda 56, 57
Cliff, Clarice 10, 22–25,
    26, 27, 42, 44, 46
Cooper, Susie 26–29, 47
Cousteau, Jacques 33
Crofts, Eva 46
Crown Devon 20, 30
Crown Works, Burslem
    47
Cubism 8, 14, 23, 26, 50

D, E

Dakon, Stefan 37
Deck, Theodore 53
Denmark 61
Doccia factory see Ginori
Dorset 56
earthenware 14, 48, 55, 57
Edward VIII 63
Etling 40
Everett, John 46

F

Fairyland Lustre 20, 74
Fennemore, Thomas
    Acland 42
Fielding & Co., S. see
    Crown Devon
Florence 36
Foley China see Brain &
    Co.
Foley Wileman 66
Forsyth, Gordon 46
Forsyth, Moira 46
France 48, 49, 52, 53, 64
French porcelain 32–33
Futurism 8, 14

G

German pottery 34
German stoneware 35
Germany 14, 48, 52
Ginori 36
Goldscheider 31, 37–38
Gould, Sir Francis
    Carruthers 39
Granger, Geneviève 40
Grant, Duncan 46
Gray, A.E. & Co. Ltd. 26
Gray, Milner 42, 46
Gustavsberg 41

H, I

Harradine, Leslie 62, 63
Harrods Exhibition 24,
    42–47

Hatchard, Ann 56
Hepworth, Barbara 46
Hoffmann, Josef 76
Italy 8, 50–51

K

Kåge, Wilhem 41
Katzhütte Thuringia 31,
    48
Keramis see Boch Frères
Khyn, Knud 61
Knight, Dame Laura 43,
    44, 45

L

Lachenal 49
Lallement 49
La Louvière 14
Leduc, Adrien-August 64
Lenci 50–51, 70
Limoges 33, 48, 52
Longwy 53
Lorenzl, Josef 37
luster wares 19, 26, 28,
    30, 36, 45

M

Macintyre & Co., James
    54
Mackintosh, Charles
    Rennie 9
Makeig-Jones, Daisy 74–75
Mayodon, Jean 65
Meissen 34
Metcalfe, Percy 13
Mondrian, Piet 27
Moorcroft, William 54
Moser, Koloman 76
Munnings, Sir Alfred 63
Murray, Keith 55
Myott, Son & Co. 38

N

Nash, Paul 46
New Zealand 55

Newlyn, Cornwall 47
Newport Pottery 22
Nicholson, Ben 46
Nixon, Harry 62
Noritake 77
Normandie, S.S. 7, 65

P

Paris 49, 53
Paris Exhibition of
   1925 6, 40
Pêche, Dagobert 76
Picasso 8, 53
Ponti, Gio 36
Poole Pottery 12, 47,
   56–57
porcelain 32, 33, 36, 52,
   60, 61, 64, 75, 77
pottery 12, 24, 31, 34,
   37, 40, 43, 46, 47,
   49, 53, 54, 57, 58, 71
Primavera 53
Proctor, Ernest 46, 47

R

Rhead, Charlotte 58–59
Richard-Ginori *see*
   Ginori
Rosenthal 34, 60
Royal Copenhagen 61
Royal Doulton 12,
   62–63

Ruhlmann, Jacques-
   Emile 64
Rutherson, Albert 46

S

Saar 14
Scavini, Helen König 50
Sept Fontaines 14
Serpaut 52
Sèvres 33, 64–65
sgraffito 18, 28
Shelley 66–68
Simpson, Mrs. 63
Singer, Susi 76
Skeaping, John 69
Slater, Eric 68
Stabler, Harold 12, 56,
   57
Stabler, Phoebe 12, 56
Staffordshire 54, 58, 66
Stoke-on-Trent 19, 30
stoneware 18, 34, 61
Stuart Glass 43
Sutherland, Graham
   42, 46
Sweden 41

T, V

tea sets 21
terracotta 38, 40, 76
Thuringia 48, 52
Tokyo 77

Turin 50, 70
Tutankhamun's tomb,
   discovery of 8, 20, 52
Van Hallen, Jessica 71
Vernon, Barbara 63
Vi.Bi. 70
Vienna 76

W

Wade 71
Wade & Sons *see* Wade
Wain, Louis 72–73
Walton, Allan 46
Wärndorfer, Fritz 76
Waters, Billy 47
Wedgwood 20, 28, 55,
   69, 74–75
Wellmer, Michael 46
Wiener Werkstätte 9,
   38, 76, 77
Wilkes, Charles 16
Wilkinson's Royal
   Staffordshire Pottery
   22, 24, 39, 42, 43,
   44, 46, 47
Wiltshaw & Robinson
   19
Wood & Son's Crown
   Works 28, 59
Wood, Enoch 30
Wright, Frank Lloyd 9,
   77

Acknowledgments

All pictures courtesy of Christie's South Kensington
   except for the following:
Christie's Images 14–15; Angelo Hornak 8–9;
Angelo Hornak, courtesy of Radio City Music Hall, New York 11;
Hulton Deutsch Collection 6–7.
Illustrators: **Carol Hill** (borders), **Debbie Hinks** (endpapers).